Tarot Cards
Coloring Book

Major Arcana Cards
Rider Waite Inspired

Aryla Publishing 2020

978-1-912675-91-3

www.arylapublishing.com

0

THE FOOL

I

THE MAGICIAN

THE HIGH PRIESTESS

III

THE EMPRESS

IV

THE EMPEROR

V

THE HIEROPHANT

VI

THE LOVERS

VII

THE CHARIOT

VIII

STRENGTH

IX

THE HERMIT

X

WHEEL OF FORTUNE

XI

JUSTICE

XII

THE HANGED MAN

XIII

DEATH

XIV

TEMPERANCE

XVI

THE TOWER

XVII

THE STAR

XVIII

THE MOON

XXI

THE WORLD

Other Coloring Books from Aryla Publishing

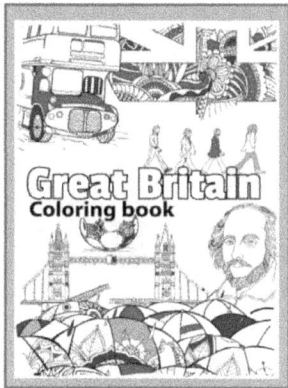

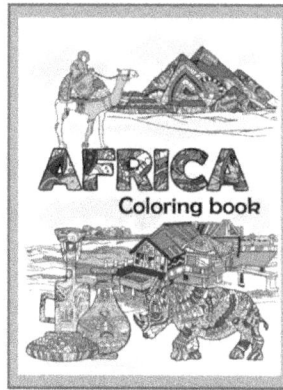

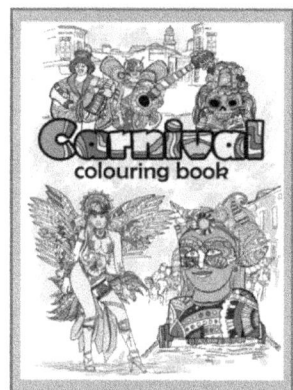

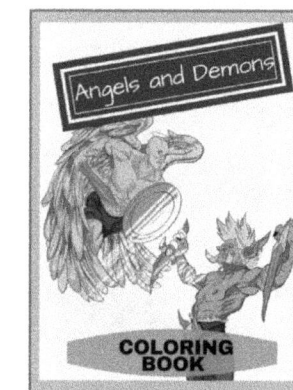

Great Britain Coloring book

U.S.A. Coloring book

Jamaica Coloring Book

Mexico Coloring book

PIRATE Coloring Book

Aryla Publishing

DRAGON Coloring Book

UNICORN Coloring Book

MERMAIDS Coloring Book

Black Inventors Coloring Book

Spain Coloring book

AFRICA Coloring book

Carnival colouring book

1920'S COLORING BOOK

Kittens and Puppies COLORING BOOK

Black Brothers COLORING BOOK

Angels and Demons COLORING BOOK

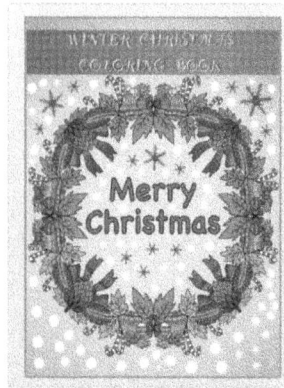

WINTER CHRISTMAS COLORING BOOK
Merry Christmas

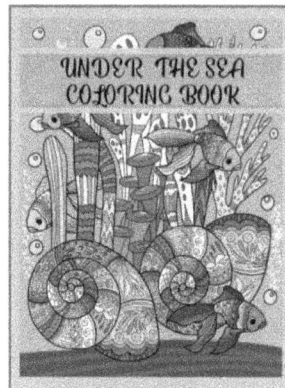

UNDER THE SEA COLORING BOOK

CHRISTMAS
COLORING BOOK

Spain
Coloring book

HALLOWEEN COLORING BOOK

MOTHERS DAY

Fathers Day
Coloring Book

HALLOWEEN²
Coloring Book

SAME LOVE
Coloring Book

Valentine's day COLORING BOOK

EASTER COLORING BOOK

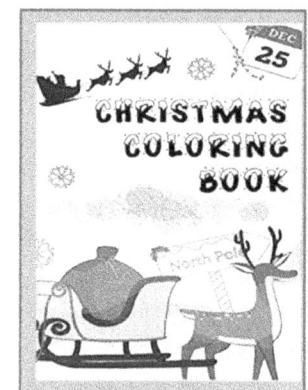

DEC 25
CHRISTMAS COLORING BOOK
North Pole

LOVE COLORING BOOK

HEALTH SERVICE
COLORING BOOK

Zodiac Signs
COLORING BOOK

SPRING TIME COLORING BOOK

XV

THE DEVIL

XIX

THE SUN

XX

JUDGEMENT

JAPAN

GREEK MYTHOLOGY

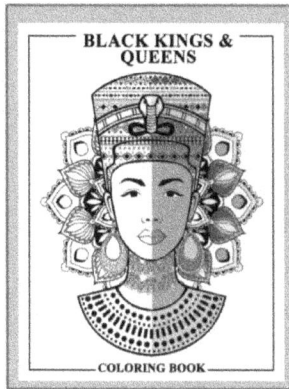

BLACK KINGS & QUEENS
COLORING BOOK

BLACK HEROES
Coloring Book

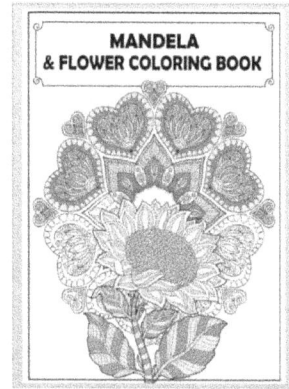

MANDELA & FLOWER COLORING BOOK

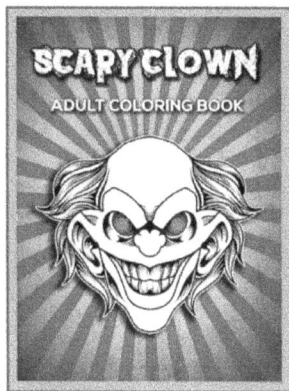

SCARY CLOWN
ADULT COLORING BOOK

CIRCUS
COLORING BOOK

ANIMAL COLORING BOOK

MYTHICAL CREATURES
Coloring Book

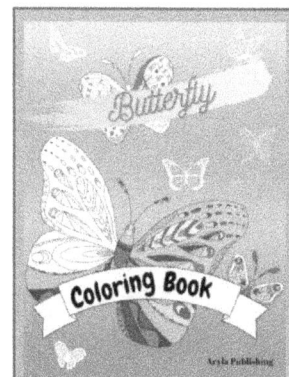

Butterfly
Coloring Book
Aryla Publishing

Color In Fun
Kids Books

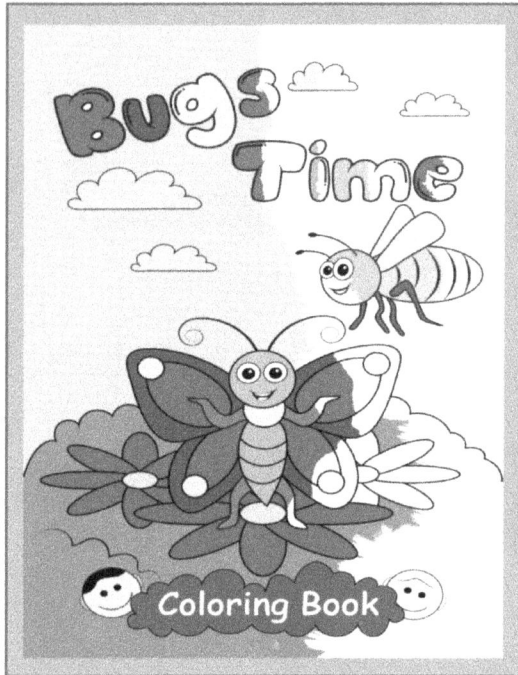

Bugs Time — Coloring Book

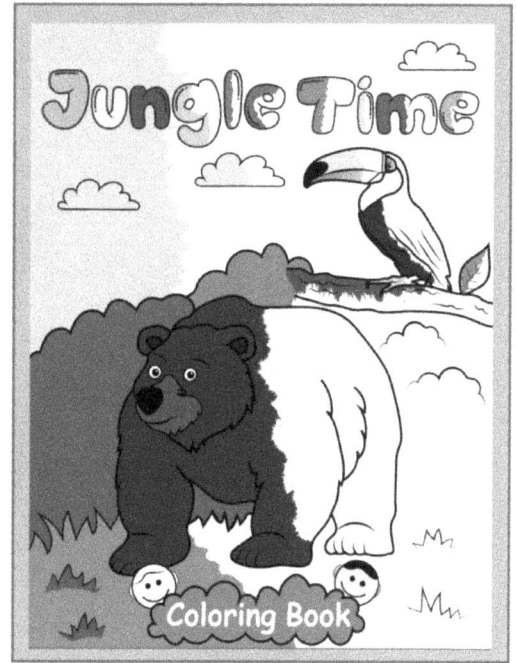

Jungle Time — Coloring Book

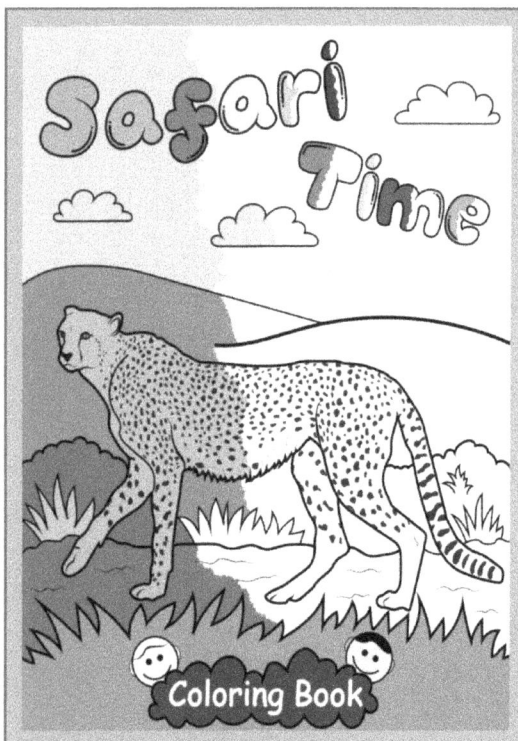

Safari Time — Coloring Book

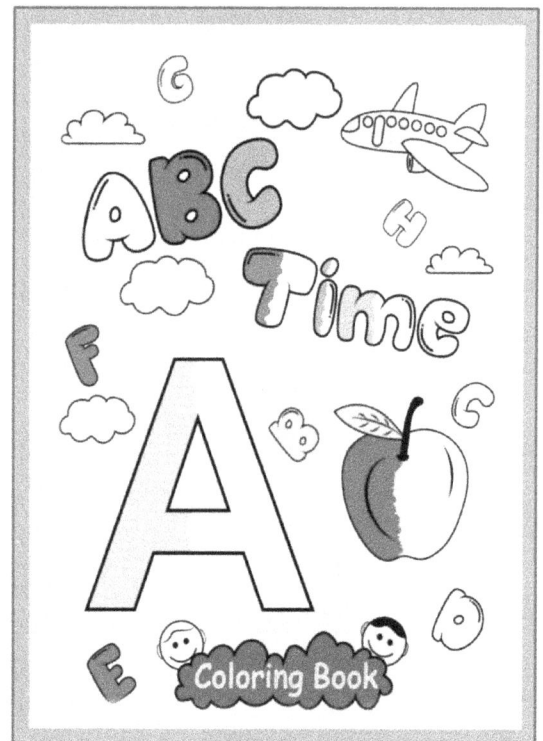

ABC Time — Coloring Book

Visit **www.ArylaPublishing.com**
to find out about all new releases.

Follow us @arylapublishing on Twitter Instagram & Facebook

Search for Aryla Publishing on

▶ YouTube

Check out our Book Trailers

Subscribe **to keep up to date with new releases!**

WE WOULD LOVE YOUR FEEDBACK

PLEASE LEAVE REVIEW AT:-

www.ingramcontent.com/pod-product-compliance
Lightning Source LLC
Chambersburg PA
CBHW081231020426
42331CB00012B/3121